Heinemann Library
Chicago, Illinois

Mapping the Seas and Skies

Ana Deboo

© 2007 Heinemann Library
a division of Reed Elsevier Inc.
Chicago, Illinois

Customer Service 888-454-2279

Visit our website at www.heinemannlibrary.com

Designed by David Poole and Geoff Ward
Illustrations by International Mapping (www.internationalmapping.com) and Geoff Ward
Photo research by Alan Gottlieb and Tracy Cummins
Originated by Modern Age
Printed and bound in China by WKT

07 06 05
10 9 8 7 6 5 4 3 2 1

Library of Congress Cataloging-in-Publication Data
Deboo, Ana.
   Mapping the seas and skies / Ana Deboo.
      p. cm. -- (Map readers)
   Includes bibliographical references and index.
   ISBN 1-4034-6793-5 (hc) -- ISBN 1-4034-6800-1 (pb)
   1. Oceanography--Juvenile literature. 2. Astronomy--Juvenile literature. 3. Navigation--Juvenile literature. I. Title. II. Series.
   GC21.5.D43 2007
   551.46022'3--dc22

                                        2006003432

13 digit isbn hardback: 978-1-4034-6793-5
13 digit isbn paperback: 978-1-4034-6800-0

Acknowledgments
The author and publisher are grateful to the following for permission to reproduce copyright material:
Alinari / Art Resource, NY pp. **4**, **6** (Vanni) **16** (Bildarchiv Preussischer Kulturbesitz); CORBIS pp. **9** (Historical Picture Archive), **10** (Ray Krantz), **12** (The Mariners' Museum), **24** (Bettmann); Digital Wisdom p. **13**; FAA courtesy Maptech p. **5**; John Carter Brown Library, Brown University, RI, USA/The Bridgeman Art Library p. **29**; National Maritime Museum, London p. **7**; New York Public Library, General Research Division, Astor, Lenox and Tilden Foundations pp. **19**, **20**; NOAA courtesy Maptech p. **5** (nautical chart); David Parker / Photo Researchers, Inc. p. **14**; USGS courtesy Maptech pp. **23**, **25**, **26**.

Cover IFR chart reproduced with permission of USGS courtesy Maptech.
Compass image reproduced with permission of Silvia Bukovacc/Shutterstock.

Every effort has been made to contact copyright holders of any material reproduced in
this book. Any omissions will be rectified in subsequent printings if notice is given to the publishers.

Special thanks to Daniel Block for his help in the production of this book.

Table of Contents

Some words are shown in bold, **like this**. You can find out what they mean by looking in the glossary.

Introduction

Finding your way on land may be challenging at times, but at least there are plenty of clues to work with. In addition to landmarks, there are roads to travel on. If you really need help, the right road map will solve your problems. But what if you are out in the middle of an ocean? Or flying an airplane?

People first started pondering this problem thousands of years ago, when they began exploring the seas. And they found solutions. More than 4,000 years ago, the Egyptians and Cretans traded goods by sea. The Phoenicians had made their way from the Mediterranean up to England by 600 AD. Two hundred years before that, sailors from the islands in the South Pacific traveled more than 2,000 miles to land in Hawaii. All of these explorers figured out how to get where they wanted to go by using lots of different clues. This process of planning and following a course from one place to another is called navigation.

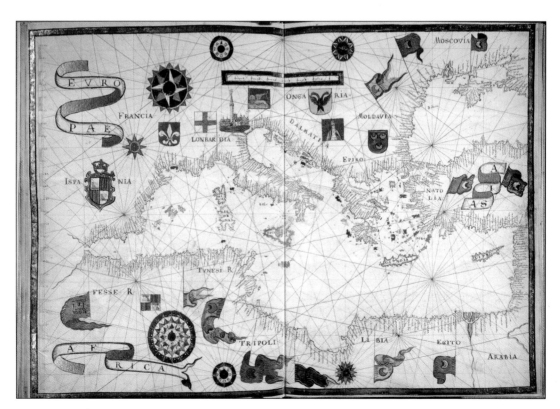

Portolan Chart.

Maps can show many different types of information. These are some of the maps you will learn about in this book.

Nautical Chart.

The word *navigation* literally means "ship driving," but it applies to getting around in airplanes and on land as well. The earliest forms of navigation involved careful observation of natural phenomena. Sailors stayed close enough to land that they could either follow the coastline or see evidence—such as a log floating in the water—that they were near it. The direction of the winds also provided helpful information. To travel farther from shore, they looked to the Sun and stars to figure out where they were.

With no more than these clues, some clever tools, and mathematical methods for analyzing them, explorers traveled across entire oceans. They mapped nearly the entire world. Later, the invention of increasingly sophisticated scientific instruments made navigation much easier.

In this book, you will learn about navigation from the early days to the present. And you will take a look at a few of the maps people use to find their way by boat or airplane. These **charts**—maps made especially for navigating—are fairly different from land maps. But there are similarities, too. If you know how to read them, they can lead you off to adventures at sea or in the sky, and they will help bring you home safely again.

Aeronautical Chart.

The Early Days of Navigation

When people first began sailing the seas, they always kept the coastline within view in order to know where they were. This usually meant going out in a boat only during the daytime. Sailors drew what they saw and made notes about the distances between places. They wrote out detailed lists to help others navigate the same area. This type of list, which the ancient Romans called a periplus, included landmarks, hazards like dangerous rocks or reefs, and good places to anchor.

Over time, sailors discovered that even farther out at sea, various clues suggested which way to travel to reach land. For example, a leafy stick floating in the water had probably fallen off a tree that was not too far away. Seabirds flying overhead with food in their mouths were likely heading back toward land. Some sailors took along land birds on their trips and kept them hungry so that when they were released, they flew straight toward land to find food.

Homer's *The Odyssey* is a famous Greek epic poem about one man's journey's at sea. Homer is believed to have lived in the eighth or ninth century BC.

During the 1850s on the Mississippi River, sailors used old-fashioned words to call out water depths. For example, the word "twain" meant two depths. Sailors would cry out "by the mark twain!" to signal that the boat was in shallow water. This is where the author Mark Twain got his pen name.

The seabed provided helpful land-finding clues, too. Generally, as the shore got closer, the water got shallower. Sailors measured water depth using a lead line, a long rope with a lead weight tied to the end to make it sink. The rope was knotted at regular intervals to mark how far into the water the weight had gone. At times, sailors could also estimate how far they had to go by examining what kind of mud was in the seabed at that spot.

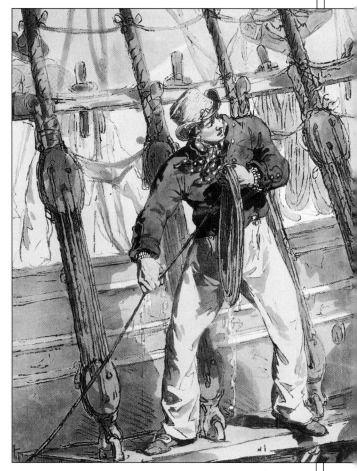

There were also meteorological (weather-related) clues to study. Clouds tend to form in a certain shape over land and reflect the color of what lies beneath them. If a sailor spotted these types of clouds in the distance, he could turn his boat in that direction to head toward land. One of the most helpful meteorological clues was the wind. People had observed that the winds were fairly constant in both temperature and direction during certain times of the year. This helped sailors determine direction. For example, if sailors felt a warm wind, they would know that it was coming from the south, and could change their course accordingly.

Measuring Ocean Depth

The unit sailors use for measuring water depth is a **fathom**, which is six feet. "Fathom" comes from an Old English word that means "two outstretched arms," which is how they created the unit of measurement. The length of a large man's arm span is about six feet.

Finding Your Way on the Open Sea

As sailors became more familiar with the clues that helped them find their way, three main navigation techniques evolved—**piloting** (or coastal navigation), **dead reckoning**, and **celestial navigation**. Each technique involves different tools and methods, and it might be necessary to use them all during the course of a journey.

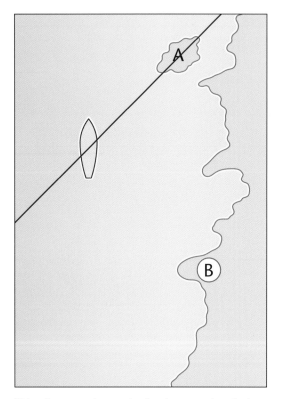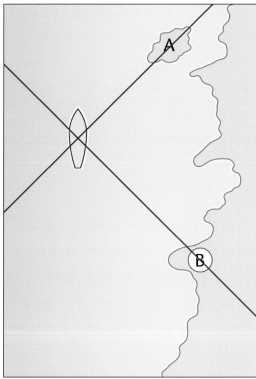

This diagram shows the basic steps in piloting.

Piloting is the technique of using a chart, a compass, and landmarks to determine your **bearings**. It is still used by sea captains who guide ships into rivers, such as the Mississippi, and through dangerous coastal areas, such as the mouth of the Columbia River in the Pacific Northwest. Piloting can only be used if land is visible. First the sailor picks a landmark on shore that also appears on the sailor's chart. Then he or she draws a line on the chart from the landmark on shore to the boat. He or she then chooses another landmark and draws another line from the landmark to the boat. The point at which these two lines intersect on the chart marks the position of the boat. Piloting requires a knowledge of geometry and how to measure angles to get an accurate reading, and it can be tough for beginning sailors.

At first, sailors used natural landmarks, like cliffs, for piloting. As time passed, artificial landmarks were created to help ships' pilots do their work. Lighthouses are tall, lit towers built right at the edge of the land. Each lighthouse in a given area looks different and flashes a different pattern of lights. These clues help sailors identify lighthouses from a distance. Buoys are floating landmarks—manmade markers that indicate such things as the path a ship should follow through the water and the location of underwater hazards, such as sandbars and rocks.

Dead reckoning involves planning what direction to travel in and keeping track of your ship's speed to estimate your position along a route. In the early days of navigation, this method was often used, but there is a lot that could go wrong. Ocean currents and winds could cause the ship to drift off the planned course, and in the past it was difficult to get an accurate idea of a ship's speed.

The first known lighthouse was completed in about 280 BC in Egypt. It was called Pharos of Alexandria, and was one of the Seven Wonders of the World.

One early way to measure speed was a method called the Dutchman's log. A floating object was thrown off the front (or bow) of the ship. Then sailors measured the time it took for the object to pass the back of the boat (or stern). Since sailors knew how long their ships were, they could calculate speed by dividing that distance by the time. This is similar to how a car's speed is measured in miles per hour.

Later, sailors used a log line, a wedge-shaped log attached to a rope with knots on it about 47 feet apart. By counting how many knots passed through a sailor's hands in 28 seconds, they calculated the ship's speed. That is why even today, the speed of a ship is expressed in **knots**.

Navigational Tools

Several tools were invented to help sailors measure where stars were in the sky. The simplest was the cross-staff, a wooden stick with a movable crosspiece. To use it, a person held it up so the bottom of the crosspiece touched the **horizon** *and the top touched where the star came into the person's view. A scale on the center stick showed the angle between the star and the horizon. Other similar devices were the astrolabe, the quadrant, and the sextant. The sextant was an improvement over earlier tools. It had a telescope and used mirrors so you could even measure the Sun's position. (Earlier devices required you to look straight at the target; the Sun is too bright for that.)*

This sailor holds a sextant.

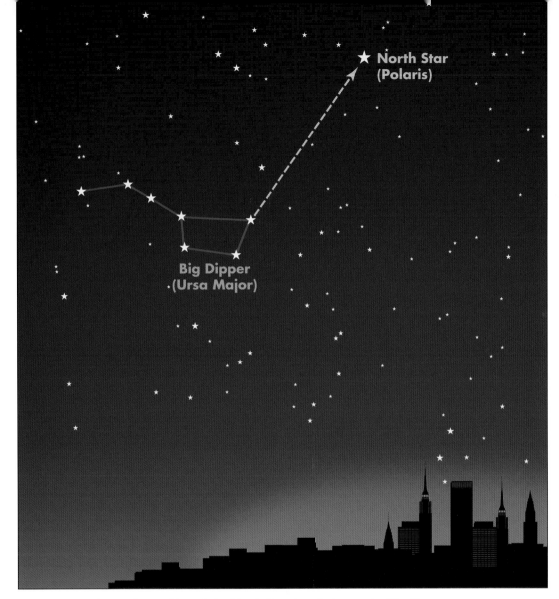

This diagram shows the position of the North Star in relation to the Big Dipper.

   In celestial navigation, the positions of the Sun, moon, and stars help
sailors determine a ship's position. Most early navigators were lucky because
they lived in the Northern Hemisphere, the section of the Earth above
the **equator**. They could see the **North Star** (also called the polestar, or
Polaris) to guide them. The North Star is almost directly over the North
Pole. As the Earth spins, the North Star stays in nearly the same position,
marking north. Sailors can figure out how far north they are by measuring
how high the polestar is in the sky—*if* they stay above the equator. Below
the equator, you cannot see the North Star, so early navigators in the
Southern Hemisphere could not use this method. However, by the 1400s,
sailors had almanacs that showed where the Sun, moon, and stars were in
the sky throughout the year. Then any of those markers could be used for
navigation in either hemisphere.

Technologies Old and New

Over the centuries, the tools available to navigators became more sophisticated. Now many things that used to require lots of calculation or tinkering with handheld tools can be done instantly with computers.

As you have read, the first sailors looked for familiar landmarks, analyzed the wind, and studied the sky to try to determine where they were. Then about 2,000 years ago, the Chinese invented the magnetic compass, and the Europeans followed in the 1100s. While it was a major advancement, the first compass had a delicate needle that did not work properly on rough seas. If there were magnetic objects around, they would make the reading inaccurate. During the 1300s, compasses began to be put into protective glass cases called binnacles. They were also mounted on special rotating devices called gimbals to keep them steady as a boat rocked.

Once sailors had reliable compasses, they could identify direction at any time. But knowing exactly *where* they were on the globe was trickier.

On ships, compasses were sometimes enclosed in glass cases called binnacles, as shown here.

It was not so difficult to figure out their **latitude**, or how far north or south they were, using the North Star or other stars. The problem was determining **longitude**, or east/west position. That is because as the Earth spins, the stars seem to move constantly across the sky. You can note their position, but a couple of minutes later, they will have shifted westward. So you cannot just sail toward or away from them and know you are going the right direction. To figure out your east/west position by looking at a star, you need to know the exact time and use charts to figure out where the star is positioned at that time.

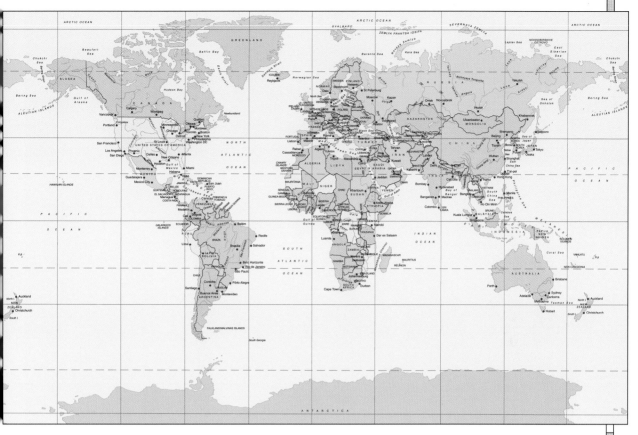

Without knowing their longitude, it was nearly impossible for sailors to pinpoint their location on a map.

There were certainly clocks back then, but—like the early compasses—they did not perform well at sea. The rocking boat, salty wet air, and temperature changes made them unreliable. Then in 1735, a watchmaker named John Harrison invented the first reliable marine chronometer—or "sea timekeeper." After that, sailors could figure out their east/west coordinates, so they could pinpoint their position on a map.

With the invention of radio in the late 1800s, a wave of technological innovation began that changed navigation entirely.

Discovering Magnets

Around 300 BC, someone in China noticed that a kind of mineral called magnetite (or lodestone) always points north/south when a strip of it is placed on a smooth surface. The Chinese later learned to make magnetic needles out of steel. These could either be floated on water or mounted on a special axis where they could spin freely. These devices led to the creation of the modern-day compass.

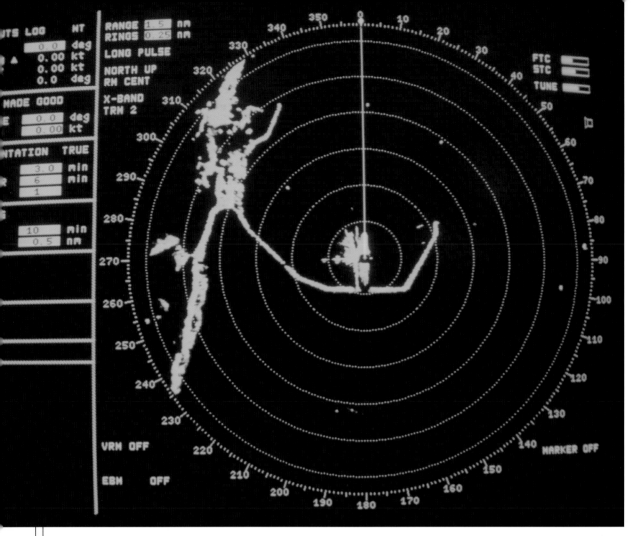

Radar screens show objects such as other boats within a certain area.

Radio technology was quickly applied to navigation. To help ships get around near shore, radio **transmitters** were placed along the coastline. **Receivers** use signals from them in much the same way sailors use visual sightings of landmarks to calculate a ship's location. During World War II, the United States introduced a radio transmitting system, Loran, that can be used far offshore. (Loran stands for "long-range navigation.") Another system, Omega, provides radio navigation transmissions worldwide.

Radar (short for "radio detecting and ranging") also uses radio. A special device sends out electromagnetic waves. These waves have a type of magnetism that is created by an electric current. When the waves hit a solid object, they bounce back to the ship, where a receiver translates the information onto a screen. A trained radar operator can read this screen as if it were a map, analyzing what is ahead and how the ship should respond. Radar is often used to help ships avoid hitting each other when the weather is foggy.

Like radar, sonar (sound navigation ranging) also involves sending waves—in this case, sound waves—from a transmitter and using a receiver to analyze what bounces back. Sonar is used in water, and it is good for seeing hazards, such as rocks or icebergs that are partially underwater. It also helps determine the depth of the ocean floor. Submarines especially rely on sonar for navigating.

In the 1900s, having explored the Earth's surface, people set off to explore outer space. In the process, they figured out even more ways to improve navigation on Earth. Satellites, small unmanned spaceships, were sent up to orbit (travel around) the Earth. Some send back pictures that can be used for examining weather or for other purposes.

Other satellites send radio transmissions designed to aid navigation. Today a system called GPS (Global Positioning System) can read satellite signals. GPS works so fast and is so precise that present-day navigators with the right equipment can know exactly where they are throughout their journey. It may not be long before everyone navigates by GPS.

This diagram shows sonar waves being sent from a ship. The waves bounce off objects on the ocean floor and are sent back to the boat's receiver, which translates them into a picture.

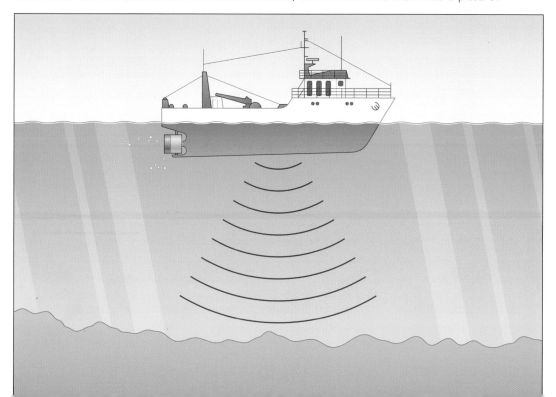

Maps That Sailors Use

As you might expect, when people first tried to learn how to navigate at sea, they decided that maps would help them. Among the first of these maps were portolan charts, made mostly between 1300 and 1600 by Italian, Portuguese, and Catalan sailors. Portolan charts usually focused on the Mediterranean, although some other areas were mapped, too. They were painted onto vellum (sheep or cow skins), so they are not rectangular like paper maps. They do have many features familiar to map readers, though, including a detailed picture of the coastline and landmarks on it, a compass rose (or wind rose, which expresses the **cardinal directions** in terms of the winds), and a scale bar. In addition, they are crisscrossed with lines called rhumb lines. These lines spread out from one or more circles on the map, following the directions of the compass. They can be used to plot a course between two ports.

Portolan charts feature rhumb lines to help sailors chart a course.

Mercator map of the world.

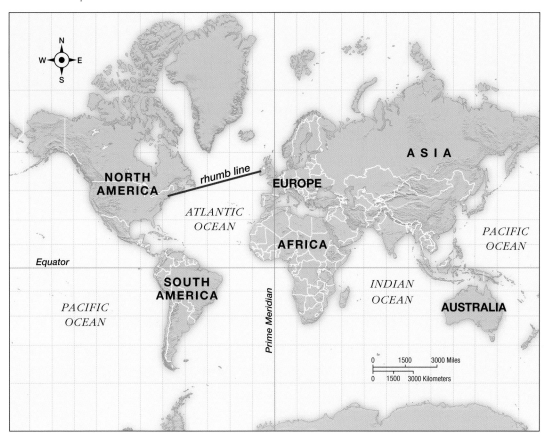

Portolan charts were not so useful for long sea journeys, though. Sailors connected the points on their charts with rhumb lines, but they did not know how to take into account the Earth's round shape when they drew onto flat surfaces. In a small area like the Mediterranean, the curve of the Earth does not affect the accuracy of a map much. On a map of a large area, it makes a big difference.

In the 1500s, a Flemish cartographer named Gerardus Mercator set out to create a map of the world that sailors could use for plotting courses. His goal was to make it so that a straight line drawn between any two points on the map went in a constant direction. These lines were very useful for sea captains that navigated using dead reckoning and celestial navigation. This meant that at the middle of the map, the shapes of the landforms were fairly accurate, but farther north and south, they were stretched wider to make up for the way the longitude lines narrow as they approach the poles. This **distortion** meant the map was not good for every purpose, but it was very useful for sailors. It was first published in 1569, and navigators sometimes still use Mercator maps today.

Mapping the Ocean Floor

On average, the ocean is about two miles deep. At its deepest, in the Mariana Trench east of the Philippine Islands, it is nearly seven miles to the bottom. The depth of the ocean makes it very difficult to explore. There is a lack of oxygen and light, and the farther down you go, the more pressure is exerted on your body. Without protective equipment, even the best-trained divers could not survive deeper than 450 feet below. It is not surprising that even today, the oceans have not been fully explored.

Once people had settled in the New World (North and South America), they wanted to study the oceans. An American named Matthew Fontaine Maury made charts to help ships navigate more safely. The information he collected about the ocean's depth helped him find a good place to lay a telegraph cable from Newfoundland to Ireland. It was not easy getting such a gigantic cable in place, and it took longer than a decade. But by 1866, people could send messages across the Atlantic Ocean!

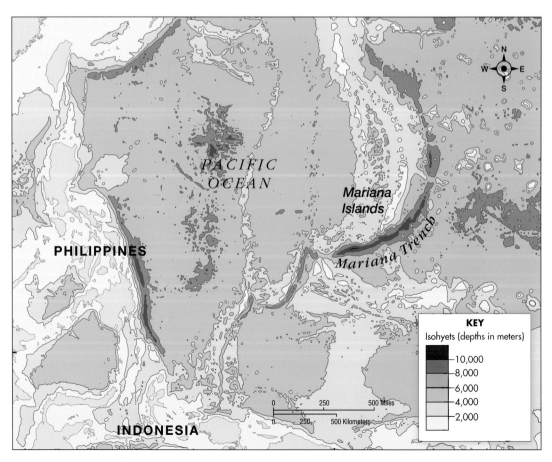

Map of the Mariana Trench.

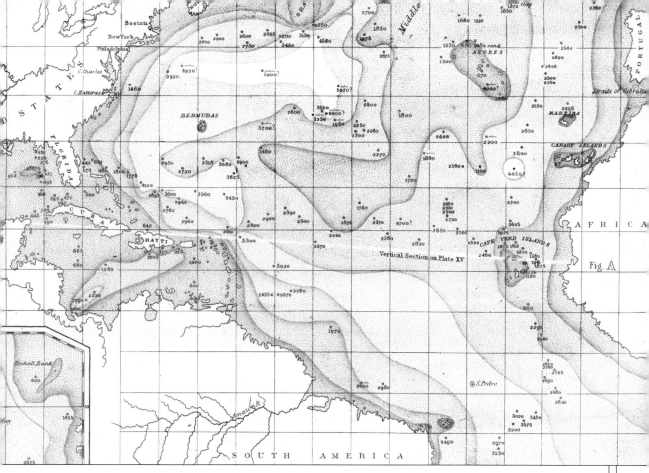

This is one of the charts made by Maury. It shows the different depths of the Atlantic Ocean.

Early measurements of the ocean's depth—or **soundings**—were made with lead lines. This worked fine in shallow waters, but in deeper areas the current could cause the lead weight to drift, making the reading inaccurate. And of course, there were not ropes long enough to measure *very* deep waters. It was not until after the invention of sonar in 1918 that accurate soundings in deeper water were possible.

Since sonar is transmitted from a boat, it can only measure the depth for a small area at a time. Today satellites equipped with radar altimeters (or "height-measurers") provide information. Satellites cannot bounce radar waves off the ocean's bottom, but they can examine its surface. The water may look perfectly flat from our point-of-view, but it actually has bumps caused by the land underneath. **Oceanographers** can use that information to map the sea floor.

Topographic maps of the sea floor show mountains (many of them active volcanoes), valleys, and plateaus. These maps have helped scientists learn more about the Earth's **crust**, which is made up of huge slabs that slowly shift, determining the shape of the land and seas.

Mapping the Ocean Currents

One of a navigator's greatest challenges is keeping on course. That is because winds and currents are constantly pushing at the ship. Even in the earliest days of navigation, sailors learned as much as they could about these factors. By the 1600s, enough was known to begin creating maps of ocean currents.

Navigators who did not know anything about wind and currents were likely to get lost. On the other hand, experienced navigators could use the wind and currents to their advantage. Matthew Fontaine Maury published a map of ocean currents in 1849. Using it helped navigators trim nearly seven weeks off the sea journey from New York to San Francisco. That not only saved time, but it also meant that they needed less food and water on board.

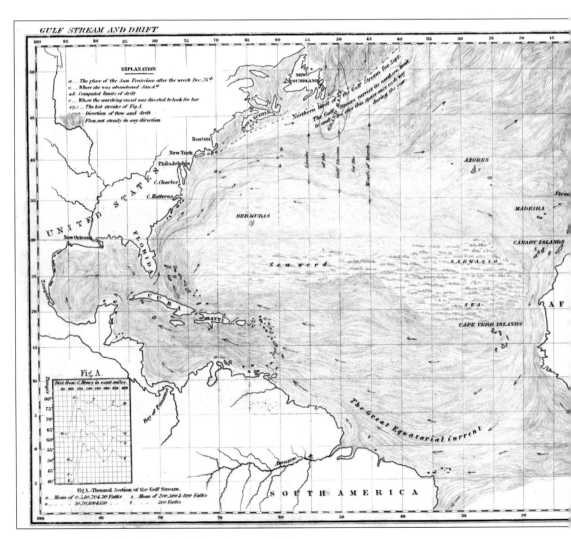

This is one of Matthew Fontaine Maury's maps of the ocean currents.

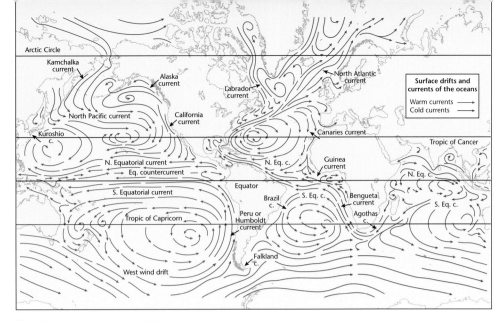

This is a modern map of the ocean currents.

Ocean currents are influenced by the winds, water temperature, and how salty the water is. Along the coastlines, the **tides** also have a strong effect. From the equator into the mid-latitudes, the currents tend to move in large circles, or **gyres**. These gyres turn clockwise in the north and counterclockwise in the south. As the water travels toward one pole or the other, it cools. In the north, several cooler currents circulate in the spaces between the landmasses. In the south, where there is an immense area of ocean, the water flows around the South Pole in a west-to-east circle called the Antarctic Circumpolar Current.

Early charts of the currents were made using sailors' observations. Now we use high-tech methods. NASA (the National Aeronautics and Space Administration) has launched two satellites equipped with radar and other devices to measure conditions on the ocean surface so weather maps and current charts can be made. Oceanographers from various institutions have also launched drifter buoys. These buoys float in certain currents and send out information about the water direction and temperature, which scientists can then study.

The Gulf Stream

Just as we have named the landmasses on a map, oceanographers have named the currents. One of the best-known currents is the Gulf Stream. It is the western part of a gyre circulating in the North Atlantic Basin. The Gulf Stream carries warm water northeast along the coast from North Carolina to Newfoundland and across the ocean from Europe.

Mapping U.S. Waterways

In the days before airplanes and cars, boats were the best way to travel between two places if they were connected by a waterway. That is why so many major cities around the world are on bodies of water. Cities prospered in these locations because they were easy to reach by boat. Inland waterway systems are not only used for transporting people, but also for moving materials and products from one place to another.

The United States has a large network of rivers, lakes, canals (manmade waterways), and coastal shipping routes. Its inland waterway system is about 25,000 miles long. It is still the most efficient way for many businesses to transport large amounts of bulky goods. The most common things carried by boat are construction materials like stone and steel, newly mined coal and petroleum, and crops such as grain.

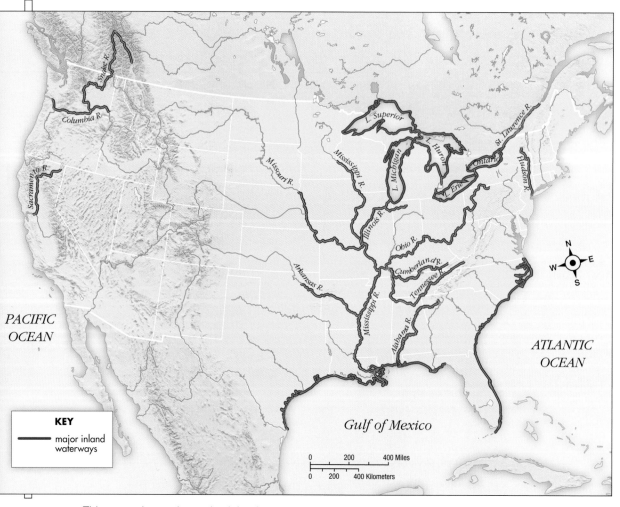

This map shows the major inland waterways of the United States.

Special **nautical** charts help boats navigate within these inland waterways. Like most maps, they include a compass rose, often printed in pink ink, to indicate north. The scale bar is a black-and-white design that is part of the chart's border. The coastline and its landmarks are shown in detail, but the interior parts of the land are mostly blank. On the water, there are lots of tiny numbers that indicate the depth in fathoms. There are also so many navigation symbols and abbreviations that the U.S. Coast Guard created a whole book to list them all! It is called Nautical Chart No. 1, and it explains things like the many types of buoys, how to read the heights of landmarks, and even what the seabed is made of in certain spots.

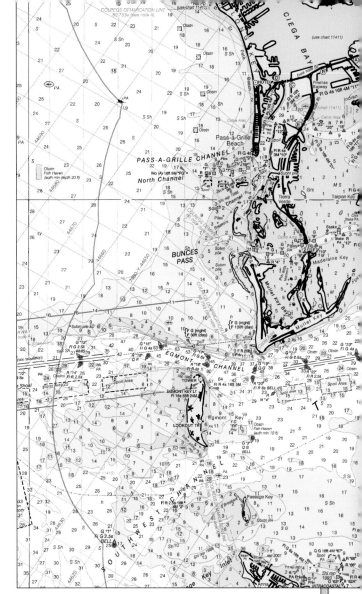

Harbor charts are color coded to show water depth. On this map, white areas mark deeper waters and darker blues represent shallow water.

U.S. River Systems

The longest river route in the United States is the Mississippi, which runs from Minnesota to the Gulf of Mexico. Branching off of the Mississippi, the Illinois Waterway allows ships to make their way to the Great Lakes. This cluster of five very large lakes extends from Minnesota to New York State and forms part of the border with Canada. Canada's St. Lawrence Seaway connects the Great Lakes with the Atlantic Ocean. Other routes in the system include the Atlantic Intracoastal Waterway, which runs from Florida all the way up to Massachusetts, and the Columbia-Snake River system in the West.

Finding Your Way by Plane

When Wilbur and Orville Wright tested their motor-powered flying machine in December of 1903, they considered it a great success that the flight lasted for 12 seconds. That may not seem very long, but no one had ever flown before. Airplanes evolved quickly after that. At the start of World War I (1914–1918), they were used to keep an eye on the enemy. By the end of the war, they were capable of dropping bombs.

Between World War I and II, airplane technology advanced quickly.

During the 1920s, the first passenger planes took to the skies, and many people got to experience flight, although the distances they could travel were limited. But in 1927, Charles Lindbergh flew across the Atlantic Ocean, from New York to Paris. It took him $33\frac{1}{2}$ hours. Now you can make that trip in as little as seven hours.

Since the earliest planes flew close to the ground, pilots could use landmarks to navigate. Even now, pilots who travel short distances at **altitudes** below 18,000 feet can navigate by using landmarks, either just watching for them or using radar. This is known as pilotage, or flying according to visual flight rules (VFR).

Aeronautical charts show the highways of the sky. Visual flight rules maps, such as this one, show natural and man-made features that pilots can use to help guide them.

Aeronautical charts made especially for pilotage show cities, roads, and landmarks like stadiums or lakes that can be spotted from the air. They also show the topography, or lumps and bumps in the land. Information about airports is presented in detail. For example, through abbreviations and symbols, the pilot can learn the airport's name, how many runways there are (as well as how long they are, their orientation on the ground, and whether they are lit up at night), and what radio channel to use to contact air traffic control, among other details.

Large aircraft often fly too high to use visual methods of navigation. Instead, these planes use sophisticated navigational equipment and fly according to what is called instrument flight rules (IFR).

Lindbergh's Flight

In Charles Lindbergh's day, every pilot had to use landmarks to navigate—at least over land. But Lindbergh flew over the ocean. Instead of pilotage, he planned his route carefully using Mercator charts and nautical tables. Then he used dead reckoning along the way: Every 100 miles, he would check and correct his course using a compass.

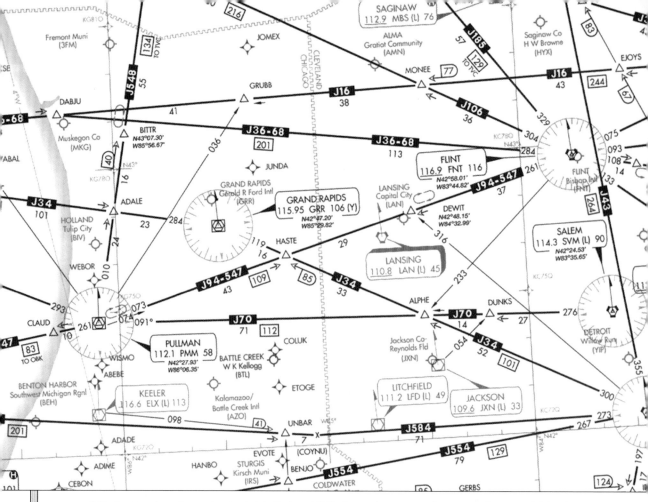

IFR charts show less physical detail than VFR charts because pilots are often too high above the clouds to use landmarks. Instead, they may use their instruments and air traffic controllers to help guide them.

Pilots using instrument flight rules (IFR) must make a detailed flight plan and submit it for approval to specialists known as air traffic controllers before taking off. During the entire journey, the pilots must stay in radio contact with them. As the plane travels out of range of one group of air traffic controllers, it makes contact with another group, until it reaches its destination. Then the air traffic controllers at that airport oversee the landing.

Because commercial pilots have the help of air traffic controllers, they use IFR charts. These are not as detailed and colorful as the visual flight rules (VFR) charts that are used by private planes. On IFR charts, the outline of the land is shown, crisscrossed with established air routes between destinations. Each route is identified by number. Also on the chart are details about the radio transmitters that have been installed at strategic places on the ground. Special Distance Measuring Equipment (DME) on board the plane translates the radio transmissions to identify the aircraft's position. Many planes also use GPS satellites or other methods to track their position.

You might not encounter nautical and aeronautical charts in everyday life the way you do road maps. They are especially made to help people who drive boats and airplanes—much less common vehicles than cars. Even so, with practice you can learn to understand a lot of the information on these charts. After all, they are another way of mapping the world—the parts of the world that are not on land!

Jet Streams

Keeping track of positioning is just as important for airplanes as it is for boats. Like boats, planes can get blown off course by wind. Jet streams are bands of very fast winds that blow around five to seven-and-a-half miles above the ground. That's about the height of a cruising passenger jet (although the jet stream winds can affect areas closer to the ground, too). In general, jet streams move from west to east, but they can also turn in other directions. Airline pilots take these winds into account when they plan their routes. When flying with the wind coming from behind—called a tailwind—a plane can go a lot faster than if the wind is coming toward it—a headwind.

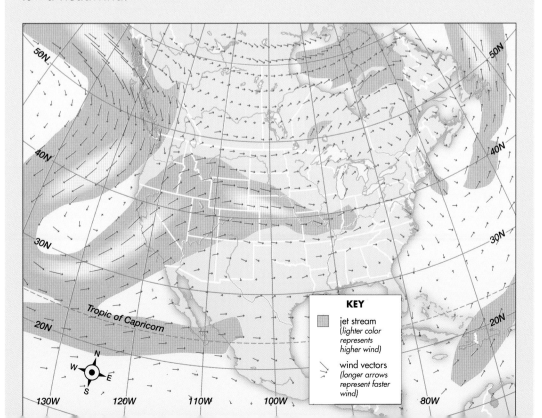

KEY

jet stream
(lighter color represents higher wind)

wind vectors
(longer arrows represent faster wind)

Map Activities

In 1519, the explorer Ferdinand Magellan set out to discover a route to the Spice Islands (now part of Indonesia) by plotting a course to the west. This was because the Pope had declared that any discoveries made by Spain to the west of a certain line would be that country's property. Magellan was Portuguese by birth, but he was loyal to Spain. Although Magellan died before the end of the trip, his expedition became the first to sail around the world. The maps on page 29 show what is known of Magellan's route, as drawn by a mapmaker in 1544 and today. Be sure to compare them so you will get an idea of how much mapmakers have learned since Magellan **circumnavigated** the world. Answers appear at the bottom of page 29.

1. In what compass direction did Magellan and his men have to sail right after they left Spain?

2. Look at the map of ocean currents on page 21. You will see that they strongly affected Magellan's route. Name the currents the expedition encountered.

3. What do you think the cupid heads on wings that surround the 1544 map represent?

Now that you know a little about how people find their way in boats and planes, try one of these activities:

• Use the Mercator map of the world on page 17 to plot your own expedition around the world. If you live inland, plan on flying from your hometown to a city on the coast, where you can board a boat.

• Take note of where the Sun rises or sets—or find the North Star using the chart on page 11—and use this information to figure out the directions of the compass. Check your answers using an actual compass.

• Have you ever swam in an ocean? Was the water warm or cool? Look at the currents chart on page 21 to see if you can figure out which current was affecting the ocean where you were.

Historical map of Magellan's route to the Spice Islands.

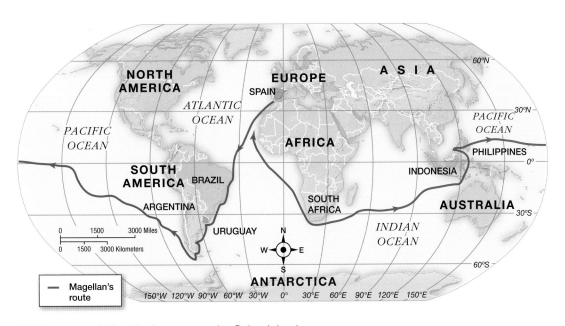

Modern map of Magellan's route to the Spice Islands.

Glossary

aeronautical having to do with aircraft. This includes hot-air balloons, helicopters, and planes. An *aeronaut* is, literally, an "air sailor."

altitude height of something above the ground. This is usually measured from "sea level," or the level of the ocean's surface.

bearing position of an object as compared to the position of another object

cardinal direction direction expressed in terms of north, south, east, or west

celestial navigation determining your position and route by watching the stars, Sun, and moon

chart map made especially for navigation

circumnavigate travel all the way around something

crust outermost layer of the Earth

dead reckoning navigating by keeping track of a ship's direction and speed along a planned route

distortion change to a map that causes its features to be inaccurate

equator latitude line at the center of the Earth that divides the Northern Hemisphere from the Southern Hemisphere

fathom unit for measuring the depth of water. A fathom is equal to six feet.

gyre circular ocean current

horizon where the Earth meets the sky. On land, the shape and height of the horizon can vary. However, at sea it is a flat line that is always at the same height (sea level). This helped early navigators judge the position of the stars.

knot also called nautical mile. Unit originally used for measuring the speed of boats but now applied also to aircraft. One knot is equal to one nautical mile per hour. A nautical mile, which is longer than a regular mile, is about 6,076 feet.

latitude measure of how far north or south places are on the globe. Latitude lines are imaginary horizontal rings on the globe created by mapmakers to indicate position. Latitude lines are also called parallels.

longitude measure of how far east or west places are on the globe. Longitude lines are imaginary vertical rings on the globe created by mapmakers to indicate position. Longitude lines are also called meridians.

nautical having to do with sailors, ships, or seafaring

North Star also called the polestar or Polaris. The star positioned almost directly over the North Pole that does not change position much as the Earth rotates. As a result, anyone looking at the North Star can be sure that they are facing north.

oceanographer scientist who studies the oceans

piloting also called coastal navigation. Piloting is determining your position and route on a ship by watching landmarks and other land-based clues.

receiver electrical device that receives electronic signals and converts them into sound or pictures

sounding measuring of water depth

tide rising and falling of the water level as a result of the gravitational pull of the moon and Sun

topographic having to do with the physical features of the land

transmitter device that sends out radio-frequency waves

Further Reading

Beasant, Pam. *How to Draw Maps and Charts*.
  Tulsa: E.D.C. Publishing, 1993.

Bramwell, Martyn. *Mapping the Seas and Airways*.
  Minneapolis: Lerner Publications, 1998.

Ganeria, Anita. *The Story of Maps and Navigation*.
  New York: Oxford University Press, 1998.

Index

Italicized numbers indicate illustrations, photographs, or maps.